Dominic and the Order of Preachers

800 Years of Service: 1216-2016

by
Fr Richard Finn, OP

All booklets are published thanks to the generous support of the members of the Catholic Truth Society

CATHOLIC TRUTH SOCIETY

PUBLISHERS TO THE HOLY SEE

Contents

Acknowledgements

Thanks are due to Helen Alford OP, Margaret Atkins OSA, Richard Brown, Fernando Cervantes LOP, Philippe Denis OP, Wojciech Giertych OP, Fergus Kerr OP, Matthijs Meeuwsen OP, Michael Oborne, Mary O'Driscoll OP, Brian Pierce OP, Timothy Radcliffe OP, Rolando de la Rosa OP, Simon Tugwell OP, and Allan White OP.

ISBN 978 1 78469 101 1

Beginnings

It was said that in the late twelfth century St Dominic's mother Jane dreamt of giving birth to a dog with a blazing firebrand in its mouth. Her future son was to set the world alight by his preaching. It was certainly an apt image. St Dominic grew up to found an international Order of Preachers. Known colloquially after their founder as Dominicans, their Latin name was easily heard as *Domini canes,* dogs of the Lord. The pun stuck, and the dog with a torch in its mouth became an enduring symbol of their mission to preach and teach the Catholic Faith. Modern-day visitors to the priory of Santa Maria Novella in Florence can see the great fourteenth-century fresco of the Church Militant by Andrea di Bonaiuto. Often referred to as the *Way of Truth*, it portrays friars administering the sacraments and teaching surrounded by a pack of black-and-white hunting dogs who stand for the whole Order committed to the truth of the Gospel. This booklet outlines major episodes in the Order's story from its origins in medieval France to its contemporary mission across the globe, but with an eye to the particular history of the Order in the English-speaking world.

Spanish beginnings

St Dominic was born sometime around 1174 in the Spanish village of Caleruega, which lies amid sunlit fields not far from the Benedictine monastery of Silos. As a youth he studied at Palencia, but in the closing years of the twelfth century he was invited to become a regular canon at the cathedral in Osma. The canons had recently been reformed by the bishop, Martín de Bazan, and their prior, Diego de Acebes. Here, the future saint experienced for the first time a priestly life structured by voluntary poverty, chastity and religious obedience for the sake of Christ's Gospel. The canons regular were meant to have neither wives nor mistresses. They forswore private property in favour of common ownership under a religious rule attributed to St Augustine. They devoted themselves primarily to prayer, study and the cathedral services. Dominic settled readily into the community and soon became its sub-prior.

However, in the winter of 1203 to 1204 Diego, who was now the bishop, chose St Dominic to accompany him on the first of two lengthy diplomatic journeys to northern Europe. The task was to negotiate a suitable marriage for the Castilian Crown prince. The project came to nothing when the prospective bride died, but the journeys themselves profoundly changed the two men's lives. In the Languedoc region of what is now southern France Dominic met for the first time large numbers of people who had rejected Catholicism. Some embraced what we call Catharism or Albigensianism; others favoured the itinerant lay preachers we call Waldensians, who preached radical poverty and in many cases rejected the Catholic clergy as irredeemably corrupt and venal. St Dominic famously conversed all night with one pub landlord to win him back from Catharism. Dominic and Diego also met with the Cistercian monks deputed by the pope to win people back to the Church. From these encounters Dominic gained a new-found dedication to preaching.

A preaching mission in the Languedoc

There was an attractive simplicity to the Cathars and Waldensians. Cathars saw themselves as the 'good Christians'. Worship centred on the home, where they prayed the Our Father and read the New Testament. The men and women who served as ministers or *perfecti* gave themselves "to God and the Gospel". They abstained from sex and fasted to express their total dedication. Yet, Catharism also had a dark side: some saw the God of the New Testament opposed by the Old Testament God who had made this world as a trap. Our very bodies were traps; the real person was the spirit trapped inside. Sex was an evil, not a good that might be sanctified in marriage or sacrificed for a higher cause. For different reasons Cathars and Waldensians rejected the Church's central sacraments of Baptism and the Eucharist. St Dominic saw how far this fell short of the Gospel to which these dissidents laid claim; but what could be done?

The Cistercians enjoyed widespread respect among Europe's nobility for their strict religious observance and meditations on Sacred Scripture. Yet earlier missions against heresy had achieved little. Even St Bernard of Clairvaux, the most famous preacher of his day, had been taunted for riding round on his high horse. Noblemen had ostentatiously walked out of church when he rose to preach. Dominic and Diego tried to establish a longer-term preaching campaign. They debated with leading Cathars. In 1206 they founded a convent at Prouilhe for women who had converted from Catharism, and which could serve as the centre for a more settled mission. Yet, the bishop died at Christmas 1207 on a visit to his diocese. Dominic himself returned for a time to Osma and was probably there in 1209, when others launched a violent crusade against the Cathars in the Languedoc.

Fraternity and brotherhood

Undeterred by the violence, St Dominic returned to live and preach in the region. Over time he saw what he could take from the Cistercians, from Catharism and the Waldensians, and what else had to change. His preaching would win credence first by his understanding of Scripture; the saint was said to have known by heart Matthew's Gospel and Paul's letters. He also required manifest humility, and

Bust of St Dominic in Bologna, based on a modern study of his skull.

a visible poverty, so he would walk from town to town, not ride on horseback. St Dominic himself went barefoot in the countryside. He would engage individuals in conversation. He would be a compassionate listener. The saint's companions later remembered how readily he shared their sorrows and comforted them in times of difficulty. Much patience was required and the records of the later canonisation process amply attest St Dominic's patience with his brethren as well as with the Cathars! He would live as a brother or friar in a fraternal community of fellow preachers known in the vicinity for their ascetic lifestyle and learning (Dominic refused on several occasions to be made a bishop). Their buildings, including the churches, would avoid ostentation. Furthermore, these brothers would beg for what they needed. The common ownership of the monks and canons depended on sizeable landholdings or rental income. This would have to be replaced by a more radical and visible form of dependency on God's providence: *mendicancy*, the begging practised by St Francis. Finally, the preacher's mission would be linked to reconciling sinners to God and his Church through hearing confessions.

By 1215 St Dominic had formed a small brotherhood of preachers around him in Toulouse. He was supported by the city's bishop, Fulk, who licensed the mission of "Brother Dominic and his companions" in his diocese to "go on foot in evangelical poverty and preach the word of

Gospel truth". A year later they had gained papal protection as canons under the Rule of St Augustine, to which they added customs taken from the Premonstratensians. They had a convent (St Romain) which they could adapt to their needs. In January 1217 Pope Honorius recognised them as preachers in the region. However, when the political situation there worsened, Dominic took the next radical step of his career. On the Feast of the Assumption (15th August), 1217, Dominic broke up the community. Against the wishes of Bishop Fulk, he sent friars north to Paris and south into Spain. He himself headed for the papal court in Italy to gain the decrees needed to promote a wider mission. A diocesan institute was transformed into the nucleus of an international order of preachers who were no longer tied for life to a particular religious house or diocese.

From Toulouse to Tbilisi

On the Feast of the Assumption in 1221 thirteen seasoned travellers first glimpsed the church towers and castle battlements of Oxford. They, too, were Dominican Friars, sent by St Dominic and the brethren who had assembled at Pentecost that year in Bologna. Led by Gilbert de Fresnay, the thirteen had landed near Canterbury, and had then walked up to London; but Oxford was their strategic goal. The town enjoyed a growing reputation as a centre of theological learning. Here, they might gain well-educated recruits and train future preachers. Within a few years they would outgrow their first house, and by the end of the century a much larger convent had been built on meadows near the river. It could accommodate over a hundred friars from different parts of Europe.

The friars' dispatch to Oxford from Bologna tells us much about the nascent Order. St Dominic had recognised the value of an assembly or 'General Chapter' along Cistercian lines, which could legislate for the whole Order, evolve a set of constitutions which adapted inherited customs and command the obedience of every friar, including himself as Master of the Order. It was a General Chapter that sent Gilbert to found a house at Oxford. The same assembly also saw the need to group convents into regional units or 'provinces' overseen by a Provincial. When St Dominic died at the end of 1221, there was an evolving structure in place to elect his successor (Blessed Jordan of Saxony), to define his powers and to keep the mission on track.

Studies in theology

Oxford also indicates the importance attached to theology. The first-ever General Chapter (held a year earlier) had probably determined that every house should contain at least one friar capable of teaching theology to new recruits and others. This required access to centres where the more capable friars could first study at an advanced level. Bologna was one such place, Paris another. Oxford made a third house in cities where medieval universities were emerging from older monastic and cathedral schools. Other early foundations would be made in Salamanca, where Alfonso IX of León established a university college in 1218, and Naples, where a similar *studium* was created by the Emperor Frederick II in 1224. To make the most of these opportunities, and to ensure that this academic labour was not wasted, the Order adopted a startling principle of dispensation: superiors could dispense a brother from this or that religious duty to free him up for study or for active ministry. Furthermore, the failure to observe what was set in the constitutions was not in itself a sin (as the constitutions themselves soon stated). This gave the friars an exceptional flexibility.

The English mission was part of a larger push to establish bridge-heads in far-flung parts of Christendom and beyond. The Chapter of 1221 sent friars east to Hungary, north to Denmark and Poland. Local superiors like Gilbert then oversaw further foundations. Dominican houses opened at London by 1224, Norwich in 1226, York a year later and at Bristol by 1230. By mid century there were twenty-four houses in England (where they would much later come to be known as 'priories' because governed by a prior). Meanwhile, friars from England founded priories at Dublin and Drogheda in 1224, and a further four in Ireland by the end of the decade. They soon had one at Cardiff in Wales, and at least five in Scotland by 1250. It was a similar story of rapid growth elsewhere. There was a house in Constantinople by 1233. Within a few decades of its foundation the Order already stretched across Christendom from Tralee in the west of Ireland to Tbilisi in Georgia on the eastern side of the Black Sea. By the early fourteenth century there were some five hundred and ninety priories organised into eighteen provinces.

Responding to need: patrons and a public audience

What explains this growth? Leading churchmen and nobles recognised the urgent need for theologically literate preachers who could also administer the sacraments. The friars could explain the doctrinal and moral significance of the Gospel to a fast-rising urban population better educated than ever before. The Fourth Lateran Council of 1215 had acknowledged the bishops' inability to meet this need. It required them to appoint suitable assistants to preach and hear confessions. All adult Catholics were now meant to confess their sins at least once a year. So, popes, many bishops and wealthy lay men and women supported the friars. At the same time, the friars' preaching struck a deep chord with numerous clerics and clerical students, some of whom swelled the Order's ranks. As a student in Bologna, Brother Stephen of Spain heard St Dominic preach, asked him to hear his confession and soon afterwards accepted the saint's invitation to become a friar. David MacKelly was Dean of Cashel when he joined the Dominicans in Cork in ca 1230.

Popes issued decrees which recommended the friars, rewarded their supporters or exempted the friars from restrictions imposed by other clerics who felt threatened by the new arrivals. In Scotland, a papal indulgence promoted the building of a priory at Glasgow. Bishops invited the friars to their diocese, as happened at Basle in 1233. Robert Grosseteste, Bishop of Lincoln, took teams of Dominican and Franciscan friars on his visitation of the vast diocese. They preached to the laity and heard confessions while he addressed the clergy. Royal and aristocratic benefactors granted land and the materials required for building on it. Two major donors, Isabel de Bolbec, Countess of Oxford, and Walter Mauclerc, the Bishop of Carlisle, enabled the friars to construct their second priory at Oxford. The bishop became a friar there shortly before his death in 1248. King Henry III confirmed the grants of land and donated timber. The first London priory at Holborn occupied a suburban site given before 1224 by the Justiciar and Earl of Kent Hubert de Burgh. Here, too, the friars enjoyed royal favour: Henry III once gave them eighty habits and pairs of shoes for Christmas. Queen Eleanor of Provence gave lands to endow Guildford priory in 1275; Edmund, Earl of Cornwall, donated land for the Chichester house in 1284.

Medieval Dominicans at Work

How did the friars go about their mission? They preached not only inside their churches but also in the squares that were constructed next to the church in some Italian cities. At Florence, the civic authorities greatly enlarged the piazza next to Santa Maria Novella. A fifteenth-century painting by Bartolomeo degli Erri now in the Ashmolean Museum at Oxford shows St Vincent Ferrer in such a setting. The painter's brother Agnolo depicted a similar scene in a painting now at the National Gallery of Art in Washington. English friars likewise often addressed large audiences from a cross in their churchyards (as at London, Hereford and Bristol). Although some sermons to clergymen were delivered in Latin, most preaching was in the local vernaculars. The General Chapter of 1236 enjoined that "in all provinces and convents the friars should learn the languages of their neighbours."

The friars commonly took to the road in pairs (the companion was known as a *socius*) and preached in other churches and towns than their own. Most kept within a certain area assigned to their priory. A few were licensed to preach anywhere within the province. This outreach greatly increased the Dominicans' audience, and claimed an evangelical precedent: the Lord himself sent out the twelve apostles 'two by two' (*Mk* 6:7). It was still contentious. Respectable religious belonged inside their cloister, not on the open road. Early tales reflect the friars' concern at hostile comment. That is no doubt why Humbert of Romans (Master of the Order from 1254 to 1263) told the story of a Cistercian monk who became a Dominican friar. Here was someone who could compare the two vocations. He said that he suffered in a few days on the road as a friar far more than during his whole time as a monk. Humbert concluded that preaching was a more worthy choice than fasting and other forms of mortifying the flesh because to the pains incurred by preaching were added its undoubted benefits for others.

Italian friars enlarged their audience by establishing lay confraternities. In 1244 John of Wildeshausen, Master of the Order, approved statutes for what may have been an existing "fraternity or congregation of Blessed Dominic" at Bologna. Its members were to take care of the poor, pray and gather for Mass and a sermon on the last Sunday of the month. A will of 1294 reveals that men and women formed two parallel branches, for the woman making the will left a sum of money for her fellow sisters, and requested burial in the priory church. Elsewhere in Italy during the thirteenth or early fourteenth century, Dominican confraternities sprang up at Viterbo, Orvieto, Perugia, Siena, Prato, Udino, Rieti, Pisa, Mantua, Faenza, Florence, Milan, Brescia, Bergamo, Spoleto and Venice.

Fighting violence with violence?

Early one Saturday morning in April 1252, two friars heard Mass and left the priory at Como to walk the thirty-odd miles to Milan. It was just after Easter, so they sang the *Victimae paschali laudes* ('Praises to the Paschal Victim') - it was to prove a telling choice. They were tailed by a hired assassin, who fatally wounded them both on an isolated stretch of road. One, Peter of Verona, died almost immediately with the Credo on his lips, saying "Into your hands, Lord, I commend my spirit". He was the Order's first canonised martyr, whose image was soon placed in every Dominican church. In later artworks St Peter Martyr's faith found visible expression as he wrote the opening word of the Creed on the ground in his blood. His companion died six days later. The motive for the killing was Peter's work as an inquisitor into heresy.

Beginning in the 1230s, the popes had appointed Dominican and Franciscan friars as inquisitors within specific regions, most notably in the Languedoc and Lombardy. They preached against heresy, but also interrogated and prosecuted suspects. Those who showed remorse received ecclesiastical penalties. Recalcitrant reoffenders were handed over to the secular authorities for execution. From the perspective of modern Church teaching on religious freedom, this must be judged a savage perversion of the friars' mission to preach Christ crucified.

Yet, in an age when heresy was considered a lethal pestilence, many regarded its rooting out as a religious duty. Inquisition as a juridical process informed by Roman law was seen by many as an advance on mob violence. A month after Peter's assassination, Pope Innocent IV urged that relapsed heretics were to be burnt at the stake as decreed by the Emperor Frederick II. The friars were to report on the authorities' compliance. The medieval Dominicans, along with Cistercians and Franciscans, were also frequently used by the papacy as itinerant preachers to drum up support for projected crusades. These were military campaigns to win back for Christians control of the Holy Land or to advance the cause of orthodox Christianity within Europe. However, the story was not simply one of answering violence with violence. Peter's assassin, Carino, fled to a Dominican convent, confessed his crime, did penance and entered the Order as a lay brother. After his death in 1293 he was venerated as a holy man.

Dominican schools

Each convent served as a centre of initial theological teaching for new recruits and of on-going intellectual formation for the older friars. It was staffed with at least one friar qualified to lecture (and so known as the conventual lector), and some houses had a further teaching assistant. All but the most infirm friars were normally expected to attend one class daily, whether

this commented directly on the Bible, on the *Historia
Scholastica* (a universal history) or discussed a theological
textbook (usually the *Sentences* of Peter Lombard but
sometimes the *Summa* of Thomas Aquinas). There might
be a second daily lecture for students, as well as revision
classes and a weekly disputation or structured debate.
The teaching often attracted an audience from outside
the convent. Every priory had a library of scriptural and
theological texts; individual friars had long-term use of
key texts; and trusted outsiders, like the fourteenth-century
writer Richard of Bury, could borrow books. Study was
sufficiently important even to determine where you slept!
Religious were normally supposed to sleep in a common
dormitory, but Dominicans could be assigned alcoves or
study cells off the dormitory in which to read and sleep -
the study bedroom was born.

For beginners, there were two years of initial theological
study after their first year, and for the more adept this was
followed by alternating periods of study elsewhere and
of teaching. They could study logic or more advanced
theology at a school designated for the purpose within
the province. From the later thirteenth century onwards,
under the influence of the Dominican theologian St Albert
the Great, the Order recognised the value of natural
philosophy and the General Chapter of 1305 legislated for
the establishment of specialist centres to teach this within
each province.

The very brightest were sent finally to one of the Order's highest schools - the *studia generalia*. The first, at Paris, was soon far too small. St Albert the Great set up a second at Cologne in 1248. Oxford had already been identified as the prospective site of a *studium generale* in 1246, but the English province was reluctant to accept friars from abroad before 1261, when the relevant office holders were deposed by the General Chapter. By the end of the century students could be sent to further *studia generalia* at Montpellier, Bologna and Barcelona.

Writers and theologians

The friars created literary tools for their trade: biblical concordances and commentaries. Étienne de Bourbon was one of the first friars to assemble a collection of *exempla*, stories with suitable morals for insertion into sermons and usually organised by topic for easy reference. There were many collections of model sermons, usually in Latin, which friars could apply to a given audience in the vernacular. Other texts helped to train the friars like the *Commentary on the Rule of St Augustine* by Humbert of Romans and the *Treatise on the Instruction and Encouragement of Novices* approved by the General Chapter in 1283. The *Summa on Vices* and *Summa on Virtues* by William Peraldus (composed ca 1250) were used by preachers and confessors for centuries afterwards. St Albert produced a series of commentaries on, and paraphrases of, Aristotle's works, more of which were becoming available in Latin than previously. The *Summa Theologiae* of St Thomas Aquinas is now acknowledged as one of the great masterpieces of scholastic theology. It is important to remember its original *raison d'être* as a teaching aid. St Thomas aimed to present Christian doctrine in the most accessible way to his students.

St Thomas Aquinas

At the sixteenth-century Council of Trent the *Summa Theologiae* of Thomas Aquinas was placed upon the altar alongside the Bible, not as its equal, but as an authoritative interpretation of the faith revealed in Sacred Scripture. Its author had entered the Dominican

Order at Naples probably as a late teenager in perhaps 1242. Family opposition delayed his studies by a year or more, but he was soon a talented student at Paris where he attended the lectures of his fellow friar, St Albert the Great. He accompanied Albert to Cologne in 1248, but returned to study and teach at Paris where he became a Master of Theology in 1256. He was a prolific author. When William of St Amour attacked the friars as false prophets, Thomas came to their defence. He lectured on individual books of the Bible and on disputed theological questions. At Orvieto and at Rome during the 1260s, Thomas reflected on how best to give student friars a coherent overview of Catholic theology, and began work in 1266 on his magisterial *Summa Theologiae*. Although unfinished at his death in 1274, the work would prove to be amongst the most influential books of theology ever written. In its explication of Scripture, in its appeal to theological authorities such as St Augustine, in its use of Aristotle and Arabic philosophers, and in its detailed and patient attention to objections against the different propositions advanced by the author at each stage of his exposition, the *Summa* manifests the fruitful interplay of faith and reason. Its anthropology, rooted in Christian revelation and illuminated by Aristotle's *Ethics* and *Politics*, offers a coherent vision of salvation in Christ by the merits of his Passion and the gifts of the Holy Spirit. Through the grace of God and in his Church men and women acquire a new maturity. Growth in the theological and moral virtues enables them to live generously and amicably with each other and with God. Indeed, at the heart of the Christian religion God extends to us the gift of his friendship through our sanctification in Christ.

From the Medieval to the Modern World

The Order's rapid growth in the thirteenth century brought problems for succeeding generations. Standards proved hard to maintain. Institutional stability sat ill with mendicant poverty. Some disagreed with St Dominic's rejection of rental income. Provinces perhaps found it difficult to integrate friars from different backgrounds. In 1314 the Master of the Order, Berengar of Landora, censured Spanish friars for travelling on horseback, eating meat and for leaving the cloister without good reason. Yet he permitted the lectors (teachers) to eat meat, as this was apparently common practice in other provinces. The students were not so lucky!

The friars were badly hit by the Black Death in the mid fourteenth century. Called to hear death-bed confessions, they returned home infected with the plague. Seventy-eight friars (perhaps half of the community) died in 1348 at Santa Maria Novella in Florence. The *Way of Truth* fresco referred to in the introduction to this booklet, together with the chapter room in which it was painted, were generously funded by a merchant whose wife had died of the plague. Far to the west, at Kilkenny in Ireland, eight friars died in three months during 1349. A Sicilian

Franciscan, Michele da Piazza, tells us how Franciscan and Dominican convents were practically emptied. Though numbers recovered, standards sometimes fell. Life within the cloister was increasingly privatised. The noble-born might occupy a suite of rooms and enjoy a private income. Much younger novices were admitted than previously. In 1378 it became possible to accept children as young as seven who were exempted from the normal ascetic discipline. Meat now featured on several occasions in the year. The Provincial of Aragon once condemned his brethren as "a brood of vipers"!

The Order was further damaged by the Great Schism, which saw rival claimants to the papacy in Rome and Avignon from 1378 to 1417. As different regions of Europe supported different candidates, friars found themselves divided in their allegiance. St Vincent Ferrer, for example, supported two claimants to the papal throne at Avignon, Clement VII and his successor Benedict XIII, as opposed to Urban VI, Boniface IX and their immediate successors in Rome, until he finally withdrew his support from Benedict in around 1415.

Observant reforms

From the mid fourteenth century onwards there was often heated debate about how to organise the Order's resources, what property to hold and how. One group of friars led by Giovanni Dominici, and inspired by the lay Dominican

St Catherine of Siena, promoted what became known as the Observant Reform, a commitment to strict observance of the Order's constitutions concerning diet, common ownership, etc. In 1390, for example, the priory at Drogheda in Ireland was named as a house of regular observance. Yet, while many recognised the need for change, there was little agreement on its nature. The same city might contain both reformed and unreformed houses. In fifteenth-century Florence Santa Maria Novella was home to unreformed or 'conventual' friars, while San Marco was founded as an 'observant' community in 1436 and decorated with simple and moving frescos by the artist and friar we know as Bl. Fra Angelico. A painting in the dormitory corridor there depicts St Dominic pointing to the stark message: "Have divine love, guard humility, possess voluntary poverty. May God curse the man who brings possessions into the Order". It was from San Marco that Girolamo Savonarola preached his fiery apocalyptic sermons in the 1490s. He urged personal austerity and radical political changes within the Florentine Republic before his sudden downfall and execution on charges of heresy in 1498. Yet many Observant friars honoured his memory for the spiritual values he championed. In a sixteenth-century painting which ostensibly shows St Peter of Verona and his companions, the martyr's profile is unmistakably that of Savonarola.

St Catherine of Siena

In a society where women's roles were frequently defined by entry into a convent or marriage and subsequent widowhood, Catherine cut her own path and eventually commanded extraordinary attention in the public square. Born into a large mercantile family at Siena in 1347, she was captivated as a child by stories of the Desert Fathers. At an age when most girls married, Catherine defied her parents and sought admission to the *Mantellate*. These women associated with the Dominican Order were for the most part elderly respectable widows. Yet, when she joined them, aged eighteen, she did not at first adopt their works of charity, but became a contemplative within the home. She went out only for Mass at the Dominican priory. Eventually, however, prayer led her to attend the sick, and aid the poor. As she acquired a reputation for holiness, a 'family' of supportive friends and helpers coalesced around her. She was drawn into a wider ministry through conversations, letters and, from 1374, journeys to Florence, Pisa and the Val d'Orcia. Catherine was a peace-maker who sought to reconcile divided and warring parties. She tried to end the hostility between the papacy and the city states of Florence, Pisa and Lucca. In 1376 she travelled to Avignon at the behest of the Florentine authorities. She urged Pope Gregory XI to leave Avignon for Rome. Pope Gregory's successor, Urban VI, summoned Catherine to Rome in late 1378 to bolster his own precarious authority. It was there that she died in 1380. Her confessor, advisor and later biographer, Raymond of Capua noted that if there were interested people to talk to, Catherine could have talked with them about God for a hundred days and nights without stopping.

Over a period of some months in 1377 and 1378 Catherine dictated *The Dialogue*, her theological masterpiece. Its starting point is the need for each person to "enter the cell of self-knowledge". Here we "open the mind's eye" to recognise our failings, but also to see our dignity as creatures made in God's image. God extends his infinite love to us in his Son, Jesus Christ, who is envisaged as the bridge across which we can run to him. St Catherine's many visions reveal the centrality of Jesus in her spirituality. We are to acquire his tender compassion. So, when Catherine meditated on the verse: "Create in me a clean heart, O Lord", Christ appeared to her and gave her his own heart. St Catherine of Siena was canonised in 1461 and declared a Doctor of the Church in 1970.

Individual houses which embraced 'reform' (or were forcibly 'reformed' by outsiders) were often grouped together in congregations under a Vicar-General. They were independent of the provinces in whose territory they lay. In 1462 the Congregation of Holland was established with houses in the Low Countries, France, Germany and Scandinavia. The Irish observant houses, which multiplied after 1488, gained their own Vicar in 1496. These groupings were contentious and so proved unstable. In the sixteenth century Thomas de Vio (better known as Cajetan) divided the Congregation of Holland into the Gallican Congregation and Province of Lower Germany. In around 1530 the Congregation of Lombardy, first established in 1459, became the Province of the Two Lombardies. Meanwhile, there were attempts to mitigate the severity of the constitutions. Leonard de Mansuetis, Master of the Order, persuaded Pope Sixtus IV to issue the bull *Considerantes* in 1475 which permitted the Order to own properties. Even so, the division between 'observants' and 'conventuals' would last until 1677.

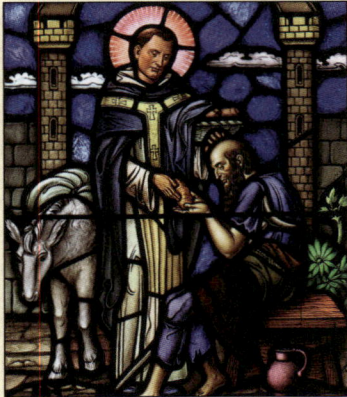

St Antoninus of Florence

Antoninus taught that only our sins really belong to us! Everything else we own is ultimately common property. Even our talents and what spiritual gifts we may enjoy are to be shared out with those in need. As a youth Antoninus put his own talents and energies at the service of the Gospel when he became a friar in 1405. He was an early member of the new Observant priory at Fiesole in the hills outside Florence. Before long he was serving as prior in various reformed houses and then entrusted with wider oversight of the Italian Observants. Consecrated Archbishop of Florence in 1446, he turned his palace and staff into what was effectively a small and austere monastic community, whose gardens were turned over to allotments. One donor who repeatedly tried to give the archbishop a fine satin cloth found it back each time on the market stalls: Antoninus repeatedly sold it to raise alms. His energies were equally devoted to the administration of the diocese and to the needs of the city's poor. He encouraged others to create a charitable confraternity under the patronage of St Martin of Tours which assisted impoverished families. Yet, Antoninus always led by example. When plague broke out in the city, he took a donkey laden with food and medicine, went into the slums and prisons, and tended the sick. The friars of San Marco, Fiesole and Santa Maria Novella followed his example. Not a few died as a result.

Antoninus addressed the difficult questions which surrounded the plight of the poor in an increasingly complex mercantile society. He opposed the practice of paying workers in kind rather than in cash to their disadvantage when markets were depressed. He distinguished between usurious rates of interest on a loan and a fair amount of interest which compensated the lender for the temporary loss of capital with which to make a living. He attacked the debasement of silver coinage when the gold florin retained its value, a practice which enriched the merchants whose reserves were in gold at the expense of their workers who were paid in silver. Antoninus became famous for his *Summa Moralis*, a comprehensive treatise on the moral life, how sin and the eight principal vices affect the soul, the corresponding nature of the virtues and the seven gifts of the Holy Spirit. First printed at Venice and Nuremberg in 1477, eighteen years after the saint's death, it was re-issued numerous times over the next two centuries, and was widely valued by confessors and those charged with their training.

The Rosary

One fruit of the reform was increased promotion of the Rosary as a privileged form of meditative prayer. Inspired by the Dominican theologian Alain de la Roche, the friars made great use from the late fifteenth century onwards of the legend that Our Lady had given the Rosary to St Dominic as a tool with which to combat heresy. Although the Ave or Hail, Mary was not usually recited in its present form until the late sixteenth century, the friars established Rosary confraternities dedicated to recitation of one hundred and fifty Aves associated with meditation on the fifteen joyful, sorrow and glorious 'mysteries' of God's saving action manifest in the New Testament. Simple piety was supported by the repetition of memorised prayers and often (from the sixteenth century) by large paintings in which the Virgin was surrounded by depictions of each mystery. Piety went hand-in-hand with doctrinal orthodoxy: Catholic teaching on the incarnation, our redemption through the suffering humanity of Christ and our sanctification in Christ by grace through the gift of the Holy Spirit. The austere Dominican pope, Pius V, who curbed the excesses of the papal court and promoted the reforms of the Council of Trent, also made much of the Rosary. When Western Christendom was threatened by the Turks, he placed Christian forces under the protection of Our Lady as Queen of the Holy Rosary. The victory at Lepanto on 7th October 1571 was attributed to the many rosaries offered up before the battle.

From the Reformation to
the French Revolution

On Easter Monday, 1534, a Dominican friar, Edmund Hancock, preached a sermon which brought down the wrath of the English authorities. His sermon opposed Henry VIII's rejection of papal authority over the Church. The former Prior of Norwich was duly summoned to London. His was not a lone voice. That same year Archbishop Cranmer sought assistance from Thomas Cromwell to depose the Prior of Cambridge, who "preached against the King's grace's great cause and most defended the authority of the Bishop of Rome".

In 1536 Cranmer similarly accused the prior at Canterbury of defending papal authority. Two Dominicans were executed as supporters of the Pilgrimage of Grace. An Irish friar, Ulick de Burgh, was hanged because he had celebrated Mass for a group who had taken part in the pilgrimage. When John Pickering, Prior of York, was interrogated, he named as 'heretics' the bishops of Canterbury, Worcester and Salisbury. He refused to acknowledge the royal supremacy, and was hanged, beheaded and quartered for treason on 25th May 1537. It was a struggle in which the friars were not equal to the Crown, Parliament and Protestant 'reformers'.

By the end of March 1539 every Dominican priory in England and Wales had been forcibly closed, and the friars evicted without any pension or other means of support. Some fled the country, like the Prior of Newcastle, Dr Richard Marshall, who escaped to Scotland. David Brown (a former *socius* to the English Provincial and diplomat on the king's behalf in Italy) returned to his native Ireland as Provincial of a newly independent Irish province. Robert Buckenham, another Cambridge prior, went first to Edinburgh and then to Louvain.

Suppression and expulsion

Collaborators in this ecclesiastical revolution were now rewarded. One, the Provincial John Hilsey, became Bishop of Rochester in 1535. Here, he made the Welsh Dominican Maurice Griffin his Vicar-General. Another former friar, John Scory, became Bishop of Rochester in 1551 before his translation to Chichester a year later. A one-time German Dominican, Martin Bucer, was a key theological adviser to Cranmer. The tables were briefly turned under Queen Mary. Scory was exiled, while Griffin was reconciled with the Catholic Church. He and another former friar, John Hopton, became bishops of Rochester and Norwich respectively in 1554. While the bishops prosecuted heretics within their dioceses, Mary established a Dominican convent at Smithfield, and two Spanish friars, Pedro de Soto and Juan de Villagarcía, taught Theology at Oxford university. Whatever their limited success, however, the accession of Elizabeth I led to the renewed suppression of Dominican life in England and Wales in 1559.

What happened at the English Reformation was mirrored by reversals elsewhere. The sixteenth century saw the Order expelled from large swathes of Europe either in the course of the Reformation or through advances by the Ottoman Turks. By 1600 the friars had lost their houses in many Swiss Cantons (during the 1520s), in Denmark (where the Crown began closures in the late 1520s and suppressed all mendicant houses in 1537), and in Ireland (east of the Shannon by 1541, and practically everywhere else by the end of the century, as the English Crown extended its control). Houses were suppressed in Norway (by 1546), in Scotland (where most houses were shut between 1559 and 1560), in the Low Countries (where most friars had to leave in around 1580) and (at different times) in many towns of Germany, Croatia and Hungary.

The 'New World'

Shortly before Christmas 1511, a Dominican friar Antonio de Montesinos preached a now famous sermon at Santo Domingo in what is the modern-day Dominican Republic. Jointly composed by the small group of four friars who had arrived on the island of Hispaniola a year or so earlier, the sermon vehemently denounced the maltreatment by the Spanish of the indigenous Indians.

Spanish adventurers and armies had been lured to this 'new world' first by the hope of finding a westerly route to Asia, but later by the vast wealth obtained from the mining of precious metals. In their wake came terrible suffering for the indigenous peoples of the region through effective enslavement, loss of land and other property, and at times wholesale slaughter. When the Indians who worked in the Potosí silver mines first heard of heaven and hell, they reportedly declined to enter heaven if it held Spaniards: the devils in hell would treat them better! From Santo Domingo on Hispaniola, expeditions were launched to colonise Puerto Rico in 1508 and Cuba in 1511. Cortés began his conquest of Mexico in 1519 and the Aztec empire fell two years later. In 1532 Francisco Pizarro invaded modern-day Peru and finally defeated the Incas two years later. The friars arrived as chaplains to the Spanish and as would-be missionaries to the Indians, but in the process some also became their champions. They articulated the Indians' human rights and documented the injustices they endured.

Las Casas and the protection of rights

The Indians' most doughty defender was Bartolomé de Las Casas, himself once the owner of lands on which the Indians were required to work supposedly in return for protection and instruction in the Christian faith. Las Casas became a friar in 1522. His numerous writings, and his arguments in a notorious debate with Juan de

Sepúlvada, were influential in securing laws in 1530 and
1542 to protect the indigenous peoples. He condemned the
brutality with which the Indians were treated as nothing
less than the crucifixion of Christ.

Las Casas's more philosophical arguments drew in
part upon the defence of human rights articulated by two
Dominican professors at the school of Salamanca in Spain,
Francisco de Vitoria and Domingo de Soto. In 1539 Vitoria
delivered two lectures - *On the American Indians* and *On
the Law of War.* The first argued that the indigenous people
of the Americas had natural rights to self-governance,
the ownership of goods and land, including sovereign
territory. Vitoria rejected the principal ground upon which
the Spanish expeditions in the New World had so far been
justified: the pope's 1493 grant to the Spanish crown of
jurisdiction in the New World. Spaniards might fight only
if *their* rights were disregarded by the Indians. The second
treatise set strict limits to lawful warfare, both when war
might be declared, and how it might be waged. Vitoria was
one of four theologians who approved in 1542 a treatise by
the eminent Franciscan theologian at Salamanca, Alfonso
de Castro, *On Whether the Indigenous People of the New
World should be Educated in Sacred Theology and the
Liberal Arts*. Castro argued in favour of the Indians being
given this higher education. In the meantime, another
major Dominican theologian, Cajetan, had published
in 1540 his *Commentary on the Summa Theologiae* of

Aquinas. He, too, taught that neither king nor pope could wage war on unbelievers for the sake of seizing land or property, nor for their disbelief in the Gospel. These theologians strengthened the hand of friars who continued to voice criticism of Spanish aggression. In the late 1550s Gil González de San Nicolás was named protector of the indigenous peoples of Chile and fiercely denounced the violent policies initiated by the region's governor. Yet, we must also recognise the support and wealth given by the *conquistadores* to the friars' mission. When Pizarro conquered Peru, he rewarded his Dominican chaplain, Vincent de Valverde, with the site of the former Temple of the Sun for the foundation of a priory.

The Order's Growth in the New World

The Order's growth in the New World was spectacular. A Peruvian province was established in 1540, with convents in Lima, Cuzco and Arequipa housing forty-seven friars in 1544. A province of Chiapas and Guatemala was created in 1551. To some extent the multiplication of provinces reflects the difficulties of transport and communication, but the growing number of houses and friars indicates both the influx of friars from Spain and local vocations. By 1555 there were some forty houses in the Mexican province. By 1569 there were some eighteen priories and many mission centres in New Granada (modern-day Colombia and Venezuela). Growth was also facilitated by the frequent appointment of friars as bishops in newly created dioceses. The first Bishop of Tlaxcala in 1525 was Julián Garcés OP. Vincent de Valverde became the first Bishop of Cuzco in 1537. Bartolomé de Las Casas was made Bishop of Chiapas in 1544, and the following year Antonio de Valdivieso OP was consecrated as Bishop of Nicaragua. Defence of the Indians would lead to the latter's assassination five years later.

The friars' work was characterised by the Order's commitment to evangelisation and theological study.

Across the continent they laboured to preach in the many vernacular languages of the indigenous peoples. St Luis Beltrán was famed for his missionary work over some twenty years in New Granada. After briefly teaching theology in Bogotá, the Venerable Vicente Bernedo became known as the Apostle of Charcas for his preaching centred upon Potosí in modern-day Bolivia during the first two decades of the seventeenth century. His reputation for giving to impoverished Indians the alms offered to the friars gave added authority to his preaching, which was often undertaken in the course of long journeys on foot. At Lima the friars had founded the University of St Mark in 1551, the first university to be founded in the Americas. The priory in New Granada was the seat of a second papally-recognised university from 1580. Twenty years earlier, Domingo de Santo Tomás had published in Valladolid the first grammar of the Quechua language and imported fifteen hundred copies to Peru where they could be used by the missionaries. By 1646 the Guatemalan Provincial could boast that his friars preached in as many as seventeen different languages. An emphasis on the vernacular went hand-in-hand with devotions and architecture in large part imported from the Old World. At Puebla and at Oaxaca in Mexico highly decorated and gilded Rosary Chapels were built for the friars' churches during the seventeenth century.

ST MARTIN DE PORRES

At his funeral the great and the good, a judge and an archbishop, shouldered Martin's coffin, but this saintly healer and friend of the poor was an outsider to high society in Spanish-ruled Peru. An illegitimate 'mulatto', a child of mixed race in a racially prejudiced society, Martin was born on 9th December 1579 at Lima. His father was a nobleman, an 'hidalgo', his mother a former slave from Panama, of African descent. The boy trained as a barber-surgeon and herbalist, learning to dress wounds as well as cut hair, before he began work as a lowly sweeper at the Dominican priory in Lima at the age of fifteen. He was a 'donado', wearing the friars' white tunic and black cape, but without the scapular or capuce of a professed religious. Nine years later, Martin became a lay brother and soon afterwards was made the convent's infirmarian. Care of the sick was combined with other servile tasks such as cleaning the latrines, so a broom became his tell-tale sign in later pictures. Hours given to prayer had to be snatched from sleep.

His care for the sick knew no bounds. It certainly did not stop at the priory gates, but extended to the city's poor whom he found lying in the streets. Martin was even prepared to disobey his prior by bringing the sick back to the monastery, if he believed it was the only way to treat them. Challenged by the prior, Martin claimed that compassion trumped obedience! He turned his sister's home into a ward for the convalescents. He planted herbs on roadside verges so that the poor could obtain free medicines. Nor did Martin limit his care to his fellow human beings. Stories abounded of dogs, cats and turkeys wandering into his infirmary to be fed and cured. In a cruel society, Martin was a sign of God's boundless compassion. It was soon recognised that his power as a healer was more than a matter of skill and experience; it was miraculous.

The healings brought fame. Had he wished, Martin could well have become a private physician to the elite. He refused, and instead used his fame to help others. He founded an orphanage for street children: the Colegio de Santa Cruz. He channelled money from rich donors into all kinds of charities.

Martin died on 3rd November 1639. Two years later his brethren at the Provincial Chapter issued an account of his extraordinary sanctity. In 1660, when statements witnessing to his holiness were being collected, the secretary finally put down his pen and revealed that he, too, had just been healed through prayer to St Martin!

The nuns

Dominican bishops in the Americas often founded enclosed convents of Dominican nuns (as at Guadalajara in 1588, or at Morelia in 1595). They had a clear precedent: St Dominic had founded the nunnery at Prouille in 1206 long before he formed his band of preachers. He had also been given responsibility for a community of nuns at San Sisto in Rome. Though there had been resistance among thirteenth-century friars to admitting nunneries into the Order, many soon gained admission especially in the Rhineland and other German-speaking areas. By the early fourteenth century there were seventy-four Dominican nunneries in the provinces of Teutonia and Saxony, with eight in Strasbourg alone. It was in convents such as these that the preaching and spiritual writings of the friars

Meister Eckhart, John Tauler and Henry Suso, inspired a rich tradition of contemplative and mystical prayer. While pre-Reformation England only knew one Dominican nunnery (at Dartford), many were founded in Spain, Italy and elsewhere.

Life within the nunnery could be far from easy. Where charity cooled, communities could divide over whether, for example, to seek or abandon a Dominican identity, or whether to accept the Observant Reform. Where standards were high, the sisters developed an intense life of contemplative prayer and meditation. At Prato in Italy, St Catherine de Ricci experienced each week between 1542 and 1554 ecstatic visions which lasted for days at a time as she followed Christ on the *via dolorosa* to Calvary.

The nuns' work included manuscript illumination, embroidery and the composition of choral music. Their studies might include philosophy, theology, history, geography, geometry and astronomy. In the mid sixteenth century, one Florentine sister, Plautilla Nelli, whose work was recorded in Vasari's *Lives*, became a renowned painter of devotional scenes. Her convent of St Catherine of Siena in the Piazza San Marco had close links with the Observant friars nearby, and their shared spirituality is reflected in the intense emotion depicted on the faces of the saints in her canvases, like that of St Dominic receiving the Rosary from Mary, Queen of Heaven.

Sailing East

The Americas were not the only places where the friars arrived with colonial adventurers. As the Portuguese established an empire in Africa and the Far East from the late fifteenth century, friars appeared in trading posts or the territories of client rulers. Some served as bishops; others belonged to small missionary communities, like the four who travelled out to the Congo with a new governor in 1570. There were Dominicans in Portuguese East Africa throughout the seventeenth and eighteenth centuries, though they generally lacked the financial means to underpin evangelisation. Few if any mastered the local languages. It was said that they preached only to the Portuguese and their slaves. In India, six friars had founded a convent in Goa in 1548. Six years later a house was founded at Malacca, from where friars travelled to Siam, Cambodia and parts of what is now Indonesia. The Portuguese opened other houses in Cochin, Colombo, Macao and elsewhere, so that by 1610 their Congregation of the Holy Cross of the East Indies boasted over three hundred men in the region. Fighting between the Dutch and Portuguese for control of the East Indies did much to damage this mission, but at the end of the seventeenth century there were still over a hundred friars at Goa, in other mission outposts in India, or Indonesia.

However, the greatest stepping-stone for the Eastern mission was the Philippines. From here, the friars would evangelise in a number of other Asian countries, though their efforts were gravely hampered by persecution. Domingo de Salazar OP reached the Philippines, together with missionaries from other religious orders, in 1581. He had been appointed as the first bishop on the islands since the Spanish conquest seventeen years earlier. Fourteen friars arrived in Manila six years later to open the first house in the Province of the Holy Rosary. Most unusually at that time, the province had no territorial boundaries, and was structured to advance the Order's missionary goals across Asia. Within the islands the friars ministered especially to the Chinese. They made detailed studies of the region's languages and dialects, and established the first printing press in the Philippines as early as 1595. The Dominican Bishop of Manila, Miguel de Benavides, founded on his deathbed in 1605 the Colegio de Santo Tomas. It opened in 1611, and is now the oldest university in Asia, one of the world's largest Catholic universities.

Benavides strongly advocated missions unsupported by military campaigns. In 1602 the friars arrived in southern Japan, where the Jesuits had created a large church of several hundred thousand, but in 1614 the shogun Tokugawa Iyeyasu began the violent suppression of Christianity. Seven friars were among those who refused to leave. They ministered in secret until they were eventually caught and martyred.

How to preach Christ crucified?

The Far East missions in the mid seventeenth century notoriously sparked what is known as the 'rites controversy'. This originated in the early Jesuit mission to China, where the Jesuits had engaged the Mandarin-speaking elite at the imperial court, and had initiated interest in European mathematics and astronomy. In seeking to expound Christianity, the Jesuits sought for theological terms readily acceptable to their interlocutors. They discriminated between the elements of traditional Confucian thought and practice they considered compatible with Christianity and those aspects of Buddhism and Daoism they held incompatible. However, when the Dominicans and other friars arrived in southern China during the 1630s and 1640s, they adopted a more direct approach to evangelise the ordinary Chinese which focussed upon Christ crucified. On learning of the Jesuits' methods they denounced them as a misrepresentation of the Catholic Faith. Three Dominicans were highly persuasive in the debates which broke out in Europe. Juan Bautista Morales was instrumental in securing a ruling of 1645 from the Congregation for the Propagation of the Faith which banned Christian converts from practising certain Confucian rites. Some thirty-one years later Domingo Fernández Navarrete issued a detailed attack on Jesuit missionary practice. In 1699 and 1700 the French friar Noël Alexandre published further controversial works. Clement XI issued bulls in 1704 and 1715 which prohibited converts from participating in the Confucian rites for spring and autumn and from honouring ancestors. The decision would lead within a few years to an imperial ban on Christian missionary activity. The tiny Chinese church, like its Japanese counterpart, was driven underground.

Surviving Revolution and the Nineteenth-Century Revival

On 14th July 1789 the Paris mob stormed the Bastille in defiance of the French king. The ensuing French Revolution, and the Enlightenment ideas which underlay it, had momentous and lasting consequences for the Dominican Order around the world. Major political and ideological earthquakes, with their after-shocks, re-configured the social terrain in which the friars hoped to work. It was not only that in many countries the friars lost the long-standing patronage of monarchs and nobility. Ideas of the citizen's inalienable freedom guaranteed by the state made religious association under vows of obedience appear a form of oppression to be made illegal. The idea of a sovereign nation state made the Order's international structure and leadership appear as a threat to national governments. The landed wealth and political influence accumulated by the Church over many centuries now seemed scandalous to an often anti-clerical middle class. The result was that Dominicans, like other congregations of religious, suffered repeated attacks on their existence from the late eighteenth century onwards.

In France the First Republic suppressed all religious houses, and the last Dominican convent closed at Paris in

1793. Napoleon Bonaparte's conquests in the Italy led first to the suppression of the Order in Piedmont between 1798 and 1802. Four years later, when Napoleon installed his brother as King of Naples, convents began to close in the southern kingdom. By 1815 not one remained. The larger priories often became barracks, schools or hospitals, while the smaller houses might be sold to private buyers. Libraries were confiscated. With the fall of Napoleon, some houses were reopened (as at Chieri in 1821), while those in the Papal States had escaped closure. Yet worse was to come. Hostility towards religious was fanned by propaganda in popular newspapers. The liberal government of Cavour in the Kingdom of Piedmont-Sardinia ordered fresh closures of houses in the mid 1850s. After the unification of much of present-day Italy under the House of Savoy in 1861, a new wave of closures culminated in a law of June 1866 which suppressed all religious houses. What remained of the Papal States fell in 1870, and the law against religious houses was extended to Rome and its environs in 1873. Recovery would be slow and at best partial.

Isolation for the Order in Spain

For Spanish Dominicans the nineteenth century began with a period of six years' enforced isolation from the wider Order (1804-1810). The king obtained papal approval for a law which separated all Spanish religious congregations from outside authority. Many priories (perhaps a third of the total number) were closed and even demolished by the government of Joseph Bonaparte which ruled much of Spain from 1808 until 1813. When the political situation improved, not all the friars returned, and the attempt to reclaim as many houses as possible weakened their common life and witness. A hammer blow fell in 1835 with a law which shut all male religious houses with fewer than twelve members. One year later all male houses were shut and their goods confiscated. The women's houses were hit in 1855: those with fewer than twelve members were suppressed, and no houses were allowed to receive novices. Meanwhile the friars' houses in Portugal had been suppressed in 1834 and the property seized by the state. The Minister of Justice, Joaquim António de Aguiar, gained the nickname 'O Mata-Frades' or 'The Friar-Killer'. The suppression extended to Portugal's overseas colonies. Similar laws were passed in Mexico, Colombia and Venezuela in the 1850s and 60s.

Recovery in France

In the early 1820s a young French lawyer, Henri Lacordaire, converted to Christianity and Catholicism. After ordination in 1827, he rapidly gained fame as a journalist and as an eloquent preacher at Notre Dame in Paris. He claimed for the Church and himself the right to preach the Gospel free from state control. He sought to preach about God and religious questions in a way that reached the heart of his contemporaries and spoke to their current situation. It struck Lacordaire that such preaching was best carried forward by a renascent Dominican Order. In 1839 he published his *Essay on the Re-establishment in France of the Order of Preachers*. It articulated a cogent post-Enlightenment defence of religious life. Obedience was an intelligent and free decision to co-operate in a common life and mission. It was predicated upon the individual's freedom of association. Voluntary poverty and chastity enabled the fundamental equality and fraternity of the brethren. Lacordaire became a novice that same year in Italy, and other Frenchmen were soon moved to make the same journey, among them a former rector of a minor seminary, the Abbé Alexandre Jandel. Already in 1840 Lacordaire returned to preach at Notre Dame in the Dominican habit. Within a few years small houses were opened (at Nancy in 1843, Chalais in 1844 and at Paris in 1845). As new recruits swelled the ranks, the Province of France was re-established with Lacordaire as its first new Provincial in 1850. Many were inspired, and not only in France. The English Catholic Bishop William Ullathorne (who was to be buried at the Dominican sisters' convent in Stone) noted that when Lacordaire became a novice the withered orange tree at Santa Sabina, supposedly planted by St Dominic, "sent up a new and vigorous shoot, which in the last few years has become an upright and comely stem, and last year bore fruit". Ullathorne hoped it was a sign of the Order's future "restoration…to its ancient splendour". It would take time, but the bishop lived to see a widespread renewal in the Order before his death in 1889.

The same year in which Lacordaire became Provincial of France, Pope Pius IX appointed Jandel as Vicar of the Order with the task of renewing the Order more widely through a return to strict observance of the constitutions. Five years later, in 1855, Jandel was made Master of the Order. By then he had already clashed with Lacordaire over the time of matins. Jandel required matins to be sung at 3 a.m. but Lacordaire wished the office to be held at 4 a.m., so that the friars would be more rested and so better able to undertake their apostolic works outside the community. In 1856, during his visitation of the French province, Jandel arranged with the new Provincial, Danzas, for a house of strict observance to be opened at Lyon which served as the kernel for a separate province of Lyon set up in 1862 (a year after the Order was re-established in Belgium). Three years after that the Province of Toulouse was also established. There would be further grave set-backs in the late nineteenth century. Friars were forced to flee abroad, and to maintain study houses at Kain-la-Tombe in Belgium and at Rijckholt in the Netherlands until the early 1930s, but French Dominican life had been lastingly revitalised.

BL. JEAN-JOSEPH LATASTE AND MOTHER HENRI-DOMINIQUE BERTHIER

Jean-Joseph Lataste and Mother Henri-Dominique reveal God's power to inspire creative thinkers and the power of forgiveness to renew our lives. In 1857 the then Alcide-Vital Lataste became a Dominican friar in his native France, aged twenty-five, not long after the death of a former girlfriend. He had earlier tried his vocation as a young candidate for diocesan priesthood and worked as a lay man with the St Vincent de Paul Society. Afflicted by ill-health, he would die young, but in the five years before his death, aged only thirty-seven, he would establish a remarkable congregation of religious women. During the course of giving a retreat to over four hundred women prisoners at Cadillac in 1864 he reflected on the grace required for hardened criminals to make a new start, and on the power of God to make saints of sinners. During adoration of the Eucharist together with the prisoners, he was inspired to found a congregation of sisters whose members would include, and so rehabilitate, ex-prisoners. With the collaboration of Mother Henri-Dominique, a Dominican Sister of the Presentation, he founded in 1866 the Dominican Sisters of Bethany. The sisters took as their patron St Mary Magdalen, who was then widely held to be the penitent woman of the city who had anointed the feet of Christ, and who had lived with her sister Martha at Bethany. No-one was to know which of the sisters was a former prisoner. It was, as the sisters still note, the same hand of God which raised one up as kept another from falling. Mother Henri-Dominique became the sisters' first superior, and was elected Prioress-General of the Congregation in 1884. After founding several houses in France and Belgium, she died in 1907. The vision of Père Lataste and Mother Henri-Dominique continues to inspire not only the present generation of sisters, but also some thirty-five male prisoners at Norfolk State Prison, Massachusetts, who form a Lay Dominican chapter within its walls.

England and the nineteenth-century revival

Jandel played a significant role in the renewal of Dominican life in nineteenth-century England. From the mid seventeenth to the late eighteenth century, a few English friars had led a precarious existence by serving discreetly as chaplains in the homes of Catholic gentry, from where they ran small missions up and down the country. Such an existence was possible because of the one priory which they owned at Bornhem in the Low Countries. Acquired for them by Cardinal Philip (Thomas) Howard, it enabled them to run a school for the sons of English recusants. Old boys regularly entered the province as novices to be trained in the one house where the friars could live together as the constitutions envisaged. This *modus operandi* was suddenly and fatally undermined by the French invasion of the Low Countries which resulted in the friars' flight from Bornhem in 1794. Attempts to recreate the school at Carshalton failed. The friars had to withdraw from long-standing missions at Stonecroft and Hexham in Northumbria, at Leeds and other centres in Yorkshire. They concentrated on their remaining mission in the Midlands, where the friars had arrived at Hinckley in 1765. From here they served the expanding towns of Coventry, Nuneaton and Leicester, where the first church of Holy Cross was built on Wellington Street in 1817. A small school for postulants was opened at Hinckley, but by 1850 the province numbered just seven men.

Yet it was also in 1850 that the ground was laid for the province's renaissance. A few years earlier, a friar in his distinctive black-and-white habit had attracted the attention of a Mr William Leigh at a service in the Midlands. Now Leigh offered the Dominicans a newly built church at Woodchester in rural Gloucestershire. With Jandel's support the friars constructed a small priory connected to the church. Woodchester was to be the new noviciate and a model of strict observance. Jandel wrote on 3rd May 1851: "Carefully avoid everything that would give the appearance of grandeur or luxury to your building: and devote your whole attention to giving it the monastic form...so as to facilitate observance and order and perfect discipline." He sent nine friars to England between 1851 and 1861 to support the project. Two, Fr Thomas Burke and Fr Louis Gonin, served as Novice-Masters, and Gonin was also Prior of Woodchester for seven years until 1863.

Universities and Parishes in the English Province

The powerful attraction of such a house on English Catholics can be measured from its influence on the young Arthur Wilberforce. When the grandson of the abolitionist visited in December 1863, he exclaimed: "Why this is more like a monastery than anything I have yet seen in England." Wilberforce later wrote: "I said to myself: Here is the ideal; here is exactly what I have had in my mind, but never before have seen in any form that I could embrace. How can I describe to you the beauty of the life there?" He was soon a novice. As others followed him, houses and churches opened in the growing cities. The friars arrived at Newcastle in 1860, where parishioners dug the foundations to save money. Benefactors played a crucial role. Countess Helena Tasker funded much of the building at Haverstock Hill in London, where the priory opened in 1867 and the church was finished in 1883. Two lay Dominicans, André Raffalovich and Josiah Spode IV, funded respectively the building St Sebastian's at Pendleton in Manchester, and Hawkesyard Priory outside Rugeley in Staffordshire. The latter was destined to be the province's study house for the first part of twentieth century. As the new century opened a province of seven had grown to around one hundred strong. Its apostolate was almost exclusively centred upon parishes, both those it ran and those that welcomed preachers for an annual mission.

In the twentieth century, largely at the inspiration of Fr Bede Jarrett, the province's work would increasingly alter as houses opened in the university cities of Oxford (1929), Edinburgh (1931), Cambridge (1938) and Glasgow (1980), and cities like Leicester and Newcastle gained universities. The province served a slowly growing number of university chaplaincies. An intellectual apostolate blossomed through the writings of friars such as Vincent McNabb, Gerald Vann and later Herbert McCabe, through the friendships developed with artists and writers such as the lay Dominicans Eric Gill and David Jones, and through the theological periodical *New Blackfriars*. English friars oversaw two new translations of Aquinas's *Summa Theologiae*, one in each half of the century.

North America

When the English friars and nuns fled from French troops in the Low Countries at the end of the eighteenth century, they left behind a young friar from Maryland, Edward Dominic Fenwick, who had joined the English province in 1787 (perhaps influenced by a great aunt who was a Dominican nun at Brussels). The future looked bleak when he was imprisoned for a time by the French, but he returned to America as a priest in 1803 and was to be the founder of the Order's mission in the United States. Fenwick built St Rose's convent at Springfield, Kentucky, which would be the noviciate for the new Province of St Joseph. He also established a college there (where Jefferson Davis was briefly a student) before opening a second house in 1816 at Somerset, Ohio, to where he would later transfer the college. Numbers were swelled by arrivals from Europe. An Italian friar, the Venerable Samuel Mazzuchelli, came out to America in 1828. He served for some years as the only missionary priest across a vast area stretching from the Canadian border down through what would later be Michigan and Wisconsin. He had twenty-four or more churches built in the upper Mississippi Valley. In 1833 Mazzuchelli published a Winnebago prayer book and three years later founded a men's college (St Thomas's) at Sinsinawa. In 1843 Mazzuchelli even persuaded the Master of the Order to approve a separate Dominican province for Illinois and Wisconsin, though this was fairly soon re-absorbed.

After the expulsion of the Jesuits from the Spanish empire, Mexican friars served on missions in parts of California during the late eighteenth and early nineteenth century. However, the Order's mission on the west coast took a new turn in 1849 when the Provincial of St Joseph's, Joseph Sadoc Alemany (who had only arrived from Europe nine years earlier), arranged for Fr Augustine Anderson to work in San Francisco. A year later, Alemany appeared in San Francisco as a bishop together with another friar, Fr Francis Sadoc Vilarrasa. They established the new Province of the Most Holy Name with a house at Monterey before moving after a few years to Benicia. New foundations followed in both provinces over the next hundred years.

Apostolic sisters

The friars in North America were aided from an early date by women inspired by the charism of St Dominic and the Order. Though some sought to adopt the full choral office of Dominican nuns, this was usually incompatible with the demands of their ministry, which was generally that of teaching girls, but might also be one of nursing the sick or elderly. At Easter 1822 nine women, inspired by the Lenten preaching of Samuel Wilson OP, founded a congregation of Dominican sisters at Springfield and opened St Magdalen's Academy. Fenwick, who became Bishop of Cincinnati in 1822, persuaded sisters from Springfield to open a school at Somerset in 1830. Mazzuchelli encouraged the foundation by two women in 1847 of the Sinsinawa Dominican Sisters. By his death in 1864 there were twenty-three sisters, and little short of four hundred by the end of the century. When Alemany arrived in California he was accompanied by a Dominican sister originally from Belgium, Sr Mary Goemaere. She opened a school at Monterey, attracted others to join her in what was a convent of ten by 1854, and then moved the convent at the request of the friars to Benicia and opened a new academy. Her Dominican Sisters of San Rafael were more than once asked to send teachers to work in San Francisco parishes.

Convents in Europe and further afield

Long before communities of Dominican women were established in North America, there were convents of apostolic sisters in various parts of Europe. In France, they began at Sainville, near Tours, where a member of the local Rosary confraternity, Marie Poussepin, founded the Sisters of Charity of the Presentation in 1696 with help from a Dominican friar Francois Mespolié. In Ireland, Dominican women from a convent in Galway had opened a school at Dublin in 1717. This moved in 1819 to Cabra on the city outskirts. Over the next fifty years new schools and convents opened at Sion Hill, Blackrock, Dun Laoghaire, and Wicklow, while at Cabra itself an innovative school was set up in 1846 to teach profoundly deaf girls through the use of sign language. Beginning in 1860 the Irish Dominican sisters made foundations in America (New Orleans), South Africa (Cape Town and Port Elizabeth), Australia (Sydney), New Zealand and Portugal.

In England, the future Mother Margaret Hallahan received the Dominican habit with three other women in 1844. Eleven years later she led a growing community of thirty-seven professed sisters based at Stone in Staffordshire where the sisters ran two schools and a nursing home. A mission on identical lines opened at Stoke-on-Trent in 1857, while two schools and an orphanage were set up in 1864 at St Marychurch in Devon. Small fee-paying boarding schools financed these convents and subsidised the sisters' teaching of poorer day-pupils. Not long before, a group of lay Dominican women who taught in a mission school at Stroud in Gloucestershire had adopted a Dominican habit and in 1860 created a convent next to the church served by the friars. They won initial recognition as a Dominican congregation of sisters in 1889.

Twentieth-Century Missions

The broad history of the Order in the twentieth century is marked by three major features: the many new missions by European and American friars and sisters in Africa, Asia and the Caribbean, together with their development as indigenous bodies in the post-colonial nation-states; the part played by the French Dominicans in the theological renewal of the Church leading up to the Second Vatican Council; and the turbulence experienced in religious life across many parts of Europe and beyond after the Council.

Four European provinces sent friars to different parts of the Caribbean. The Irish had taken over responsibility for a mission on Trinidad from French friars in 1897 (though French and Irish worked alongside each other for several decades). The English took on a mission on Grenada in 1901 which later extended to Barbados and Jamaica. The Dutch (who had already a mission in the Dutch Antilles since 1870) arrived on Puerto Rico in 1904. French friars from the Province of Toulouse would arrive much later in Haiti.

Africa

In colonial Africa, Belgian Dominicans opened a string of mission churches, schools and health centres in the Uele district of the Belgian Congo from 1912 onwards. By 1940 forty-six friars and thirty-three sisters ministered to more than fifty thousand Christians. In Southern Africa the Dominican Mother Rose Niland persuaded the Catholic Vicar Apostolic in the Transvaal to invite the English friars to the region, and the first, Fr Laurence Shapcote, arrived in Boksburg in 1917. After initial set-backs, new houses opened at Brakpan and Springs in the East Rand, at Klerksdorp in the Transvaal and Potchefstroom, culminating in 1930 with a house in the Afrikaner university town of Stellenbosch. Dutch Dominicans arrived in the country just two years later to establish a separate mission round Kroonstadt in the Orange Free State.

After a hiatus caused by the Second World War, further African missions opened in the 1950s. American friars were invited to work in Nigeria, where three arrived in Lagos, at Yaba, in 1951. A year later they gained responsibility for a wide mission territory assisted by twelve sisters who had been sent from South Bend, Indiana. 1954 saw the first friar of the Lyon province arrive at Dakar (then the capital of French West Africa). When a few more followed, their ministry centred upon the university, work with young people and radio broadcasts. 1955 also saw the Province of France open a house at Douala in the Cameroun. At Butare, in Rwanda, where four Canadian friars had arrived in 1960, a national university was established at government request in 1963.

Independence and conflict

Several missions suffered in the conflicts that preceded or followed national independence. Thirteen Dominicans lost their lives in the Congo during the civil war of 1964. They withdrew temporarily from Uele and re-focussed their apostolate on Leopoldville (now Kinshasa), where they had already assisted in setting up the theology faculty of Lovanium University. At Dakar in 1968 the friars' solidarity with students brutally treated by the security forces led the Senegalese president to threaten expulsion from the country. The university chaplaincy had to be relinquished. Repeated attempts to work with students and others in Brazzaville were frustrated either by government opposition (as in 1970) or civil war (in the 1990s). South Africa, where the Dutch and English vicariates merged to form a general vicariate in 1968, was not a newly independent nation, but the growing opposition to the apartheid regime by friars and sisters soon led to several being expelled from the country. The security forces detained three sisters in 1985. A year later, the sometime Provincial, Albert Nolan, who took a lead in developing an African liberation theology, and was a leading composer of the *Kairos Document*, went into hiding for some months. Another friar, Peter Hortop, was held for three months in solitary confinement and remained in prison for a further three before his release in February 1987.

Progress across Africa was hampered first by an initial failure to attract and retain local vocations. There was uncertainty about how to form the few men who sought entry into the Order, whether to do so overseas or in Africa. The establishment of African centres of formation was complicated by the many entities involved: the overseas provinces and the regional vicariates they had established. From the 1970s onward, there were also fewer arrivals from outside Africa to support the missions. Yet, Ibadan became an international African study centre of the Order in 1976 and in 1982 Kinshasa was selected as a centre for theology in Africa.

In Nigeria and Ghana rising vocations led to the erection in 1993 of the Province of St Joseph the Worker, which was soon strong enough to send friars outside these countries. As the second decade of the twenty-first century got underway the province numbered around one hundred and forty friars. Elsewhere on the continent there were some seventy or so friars assigned to the General Vicariate of the Democratic Republic of the Congo, and some sixty in the West African countries of Benin, Senegal and the Ivory Coast. There were just under forty friars in Southern Africa, another thirty or so in Rwanda and Burundi and a similar number in Kenya. A further twenty or so belonged to the Angolan Vicariate, some forty to the Vicariate of Equatorial Africa. Across the continent there were also around hundred and eighty communities of Dominican religious women.

Resourcing Church and society

In 1935, the Regent of Studies at Le Saulchoir, the *studium* of the Province of France, Marie-Dominique Chenu, published a stinging critique of contemporary Catholic theology. It had lost touch with ordinary life, pastoral practice and spirituality. Its teaching manuals reduced theology to so many doctrinal ledgers. Over the next decades, and often despite opposition from the hierarchy, he and other French Dominicans, most notably Yves Congar, laboured to renew theology and re-connect it with wider Christian life. Congar recalled people from a shallow version of tradition into deeper waters awaiting rediscovery. The Church was to be refreshed with new theological resources, re-sensitised to the Biblical and Patristic sources of theological reflection. This *ressourcement* was advanced in large part by the French Dominicans' publishing house, Editions du Cerf, set up in 1927. In collaboration with leading Jesuits and other scholars they began to issue *Sources Chrétiennes*, critical editions of Patristic texts in Greek or Latin with a French translation and commentary. The first, Gregory of Nyssa's *Life of Moses*, was edited by Jean Daniélou SJ and appeared in 1941. Chenu re-awakened interest in medieval philosophical theology, enabling a renewal of Thomism (the study and application of Aquinas's thought) which by-passed the manuals. Congar made theological use of the sources to challenge an ignorant conservatism. He distinguished between true and false reform, studied the role of the laity, the relationship of Scripture to tradition, the need to escape an overly juridical approach to Church life, the proper place of the diaconate as a distinct clerical order, ecumenism and the theology of the Holy Spirit.

Worker-priests

Together with Chenu and a third friar, Henri-Marie Féret, Congar gave theological support to the hundred-strong movement of worker-priests who had taken jobs in the car factories and other industries in the hope of re-evangelising the French working-class, while ten friars themselves became worker-priests. In 1953 the French bishops and the Vatican decided to end the movement, which they saw as incompatible with priestly identity and as a dangerous collaboration with communists in the trade unions. The Master of the Order was threatened with the loss of the Order's independence and even its suppression in France. In February 1954 he required all three French provincials to resign. Chenu, Congar and Féret were removed from Paris, while the Head of Editions du Cerf was also replaced. It was a blow to the much wider project of theological renewal. Yet, a decade later, these same theologians served as experts at the Second Vatican Council.

Jerusalem and Cairo

Much earlier, in 1890, a French Dominican, Marie-Joseph Lagrange, had founded the École Biblique in Jerusalem for study of the Bible informed by an understanding of the Holy Land and its archaeology. Scholars at the École responded to the call of Pius XII in 1943 for translations from the Greek and Hebrew texts of the Bible as opposed to the Latin Vulgate. *La Bible de Jérusalem* was published to critical acclaim in 1956. It inspired the English *Jerusalem Bible* which appeared a decade later. Meanwhile, Marie-Dominique Chenu had also encouraged Georges Anawati, an Alexandrian-born friar, to specialise in Islamic and Arab studies. Together with two other French friars, Serge de Beaurecueil and Jacques Jomier, Anawati founded the Order's Centre for Islamic Studies (IDEO) at Cairo in the early 1950s.

Social sciences

French Dominicans also contributed to wider intellectual and social developments. In the late 1920s Louis-Joseph Lebret was struck by how Breton fishermen's families had suffered from industrialisation. His initial response was to found movements which supported the young and the poor. He promoted unionisation, and legal changes. However, Lebret also saw the need to re-envisage social development: economic issues were to be integrated within consideration of larger questions about human flourishing. Exploitation of natural resources by the rich could be dehumanising: talk of development might cloak exploitation of the vulnerable and drive deeper social inequalities.

Drawing partly on Marxist ideas, Lebret founded in 1941 *Économie et Humanisme*, a centre at Lyons for interdisciplinary study and co-operation among workers. A journal of this name was created shortly afterwards, and Lebret developed his ideas on social geography and regional planning in a steady stream of papers. 1947 saw the first of several visits to South America where Dominicans helped to disseminate his ideas. In Brazil, Lebret set up SAGMACS, a centre for social research which would train hundreds in the related fields of economics, sociology, urban planning and administration. In Uruguay Lebret inspired 'Common Good Teams'. These were replaced by the Latin American Center for Economics and Humanism (CLAEH) in 1958, among whose directors were Benevenuto de Santa Cruz OP and Paul Ramlot OP. Back in France, Lebret created the International Institute of Research and Training towards Integrating Development in 1958 and a new journal *Développement et Civilisations* two years later. Church authorities, previously suspicious, now made him the Holy See's representative at international conferences. Summoned by Dom Helder Camara to be an advisor at Vatican II, it was said that he had the Church Fathers' writings on poverty handed out to the bishops in the corridors. He assisted in drafting what became the Pastoral Constitution *Gaudium et Spes*. Shortly after his death in 1966, Pope Paul VI named him as a major influence behind his encyclical *Populorum Progressio*.

Bl. Giuseppe Girotti and Bl. Michal Czartoryski

Two friars were among those who lost their lives for helping Jews persecuted by the Nazis and their collaborators during the Second World War. After studies at the Angelicum (the Dominican university in Rome) and at the École Biblique in Jerusalem, Giuseppe Girotti taught theology in Turin. Following the Nazi occupation of Italy in 1943 he arranged hideouts for Jews who were being smuggled out of the country, but was caught in August 1944 while helping a Jew who had been wounded. Girotti was sent to Dachau where he died on 1st April 1945.

Michal Czartoryski entered the Polish Dominican province in 1927 after training as an engineer and architect. He ministered to students, before taking part as a chaplain in the Warsaw uprising of August 1944. His days were largely spent in cellars that had been turned into make-shift hospital wards, and where he set up a chapel to celebrate Mass. Refusing to take off his religious habit or to abandon the sick and injured, he was shot on 6th September 1944 together with the patients seized by the Nazis.

Turbulence and the recovery of nerve

The impact on the Church of the Second Vatican Council has been profound. The reception of its documents in the second half of the twentieth century coincided with major social changes which included secularisation in Western Europe, and the collapse of communism in Central and Eastern Europe. The Order faced new and different challenges across the globe. One result of the Council was a large-scale revision of the Order's constitutions at the River Forest General Chapter of 1968. A new 'Fundamental Constitution' identified unchanging elements in articulating and structuring the Order's mission. The Order's government was greatly simplified to improve its flexibility and to nurture a fraternity that was not inhibited by emphasis on seniority of profession, the ritual punishment of faults and tight control of personal correspondence. At a time when the internal life of the Order was changing, and as western societies also became sexually more permissive, many friars left the Order to marry. Across Western Europe and North America numbers reached a high-point in the mid-sixties or seventies but then began to fall. A little under six hundred men, over four hundred of them priests, belonged to the Dutch province in 1961. By the end of the century the total number would drop to little over one hundred and thirty. Large study houses, like Tallaght in Ireland and Walberberg in Germany, were closed or put to new uses as fewer men joined and stayed. One approach to philosophical theology had been swept away; a crisis of confidence arose in how to form those who entered with mind-sets very different from an older generation.

Eastern Europe

When communism fell in Eastern Europe, friars who had survived sometimes heroically under oppressive regimes could again open communities where they were previously banned, as in Hungary, Czechoslovakia as it was then and East Germany. The transition from living alone and exercising a clandestine ministry to forming new communities was often difficult. Poland, where the Order had retained many houses, and a large *studium* at Krakow, was an exception. Three large provinces (Polish, Ruthenian and Lithuanian) had existed within the borders of eighteenth-century Poland. The partitioning of the Republic and a series of repressive measures in the following century led to the friars' disappearance from what are now the Baltic states, Belarus and Ukraine, as well as from Russian and Prussian occupied Poland. Many friars were deported to Siberia. Many were martyred during the Soviet period. Yet, a long-term renaissance in the Order began after 1918 led by a distinguished Thomist scholar Jacek Woroniecki OP. Recovery continued after 1945 in spite of communism. Polish friars strongly supported the continued existence of a Catholic intelligentsia through pastoral work with students at Poznan, Krakow, Gdansk and Lublin. Their publishing house *W Drodze* oversaw the translation into Polish of Catholic theological works from abroad. By the end of the twentieth century the Polish province was heading towards a membership of five hundred friars. With the fall of communism, priories were re-established in parts of the former Soviet Union, notably in St Petersburg, Vilnius, Vitebsk and Kiev.

An enduring purpose

Timothy Radcliffe, Master of the Order from 1992 to 2001, cogently re-articulated the value of religious life formed by poverty, chastity and obedience in a series of letters to the Order. In the twenty-first century there are signs of strong resurgence in various provinces as young men see the value of a Christian formation and an intellectual tradition which invites questions. The Order's relevance in an age of re-evangelisation is clear. In the United States, the Eastern Province of St Joseph has been twice sub-divided in the twentieth century, once to form the Central Province of St Albert in 1939, and a second time in 1979, with some territory taken from the latter province, to form the Southern Province of St Martin de Porres, while there are currently another hundred and fifty friars in the Western province. The Washington House of Studies, opened originally in the early twentieth century, has seen a recent wave of new vocations. At Oxford, the English friars opened a Private Hall of the University of

Oxford in 1994. In the new millennium Blackfriars Hall welcomes mature students of Theology and Philosophy, and promotes Thomism and Catholic Social Teaching through its Aquinas and Las Casas Institutes. Across the Order, about one sixth of the friars are new members in training. There are growing numbers of friars, sisters and lay Dominicans in Vietnam, thriving provinces in India and the Philippines, as well as new Asian missions.

Some eight hundred years after St Dominic created the Order of Preachers, God's dogs are still busy, active in over one hundred countries across the globe. Much remains to be done. As the friars' Fundamental Constitution declares, the Order must renew and "adapt itself courageously" in times of "accelerating change" for its "fundamental purpose and the way of life which follows from it retain their worth in every age".

Further information

The Dominican Friars - England & Scotland:
www.english.op.org

Order of Preachers: www.op.org/en

Further reading

Benedict M Ashley OP, *The Dominicans* (Wipf and Stock 2009).

Guy Bedouelle OP, *In the Image of St Dominic, Nine Portraits of Dominican Life* (San Francisco, 1994).

Don Brophy, *Catherine of Siena: A Passionate Life* (BlueBridge 2010).

Lawrence A. Clayton, *Bartolomé de las Casas and the Conquest of the Americas* (Wiley-Blackwell, 2011).

Francesco Compagnoni OP and Helen Alford OP (eds), *Preaching Justice: Dominican Contributions to Social Ethics in the Twentieth Century* (Dominican Publications, 2007).

Celia Cussen, *Black Saint of the Americas: The Life and Afterlife of Martin de Porres* (Cambridge University Press, 2014).

Brian Davies OP, *Aquinas, An Introduction* (Continuum, 2002).

Paul Murray OP, *The New Wine of Dominican Spirituality: A Drink Called Happiness* (Burns and Oates, 2006).

Anselm Nye, *A Peculiar Kind of Mission, The English Dominican Sisters, 1845-2010* (Gracewing, 2011).

Mary O'Driscoll OP (ed.), *Catherine of Siena, Passion for the Truth, Compassion for Humanity: Selected Spiritual Writings* (New City Press, 1993).

Picture credits

Page 7: St Dominic. Bust of St Dominic in Bologna, based on a modern study of his skull. © Lawrence Lew OP, 2013. Page 21: St Thomas Aquinas. 'St Thomas Confounding the Heretics', fresco by Filippino Lippi, Carafa Chapel in the Dominican church of Sta Maria sopra Minerva in Rome. © Lawrence Lew OP, 2010.

Page 27: St Catherine of Siena. Painting in the library of Blackfriars, Oxford. © Lawrence Lew OP, 2007.

Page 30: St Antoninus. Detail from a stained-glass window in St Dominic's Church in Washington DC. © Lawrence Lew OP, 2014.

Page 42: St Martin de Porres. Statue in St Dominic's Priory Church, London NW5. © Lawrence Lew OP, 2008.

Page 55: Mother Henri-Dominique Berthier and Jean-Joseph Lataste. Drawn by a prisoner at Norfolk Prison, MA, USA, where there is a chapter of the Lay Fraternity of St Dominic, the first of its kind in a prison setting. By kind permission of Bethany House Ministries, www.bethanyhouseministry.com.

A world of Catholic reading at your fingertips...

Catholic Faith, Life & Truth for all

CTS

www.CTSbooks.org

twitter: @CTSpublishers

facebook.com/CTSpublishers

Catholic Truth Society, Publishers to the Holy See.